Original title:
A Realm Untold

Copyright © 2024 Creative Arts Management OÜ
All rights reserved.

Author: Ronan Whitfield
ISBN HARDBACK: 978-9916-90-566-1
ISBN PAPERBACK: 978-9916-90-567-8

Voices of the Unheard

Echoes in the alleyways,
Whispers of the night,
Stories left unspoken,
Yearning for the light.

Faces in the shadows,
Eyes that tell of pain,
Dreams that lie forgotten,
Dancing in the rain.

Hearts that beat in silence,
Hope wrapped in despair,
Seeking understanding,
Finding none to share.

Lift the veil of silence,
Hear their solemn plea,
Voices of the unheard,
Yearning to be free.

Fantasies Enshrouded in Mist

In the dawn's soft embrace,
Dreams take flight and soar,
Chasing shadows of longing,
Whispers from before.

Veils of silver fog,
Hide the tales untold,
Secrets wrapped in wonder,
Glimmers rich and bold.

In this twilight realm,
Reality bends and sways,
Thoughts entwined in magic,
Lost in endless plays.

With each step we wander,
Into the unknown,
Fantasies enfolding,
Hearts that feel at home.

Flickers of a Distant Fire

In the stillness of the night,
Flickers break the dark,
Embers hint of warmth,
Kindling hope's small spark.

Whispers in the wind,
Carrying tales of yore,
Longing for connection,
To ignite once more.

Waves of light are dancing,
Casting dreams so bright,
Guiding weary travelers,
Through the endless night.

Flickers of a fire,
Calling from afar,
Join the light of others,
Together we will star.

Threads of the Untold

Woven in the silence,
Stories thread the air,
Each a whispered secret,
Laden with despair.

Tales of love forgotten,
Echoing through time,
Binding past to present,
In rhythm and in rhyme.

Hands that reach for healing,
From the wounds of old,
Stitching broken memories,
With threads of purest gold.

We carry these unspoken,
Stories yet to see,
Threads of the untold,
Woven into me.

Landscapes of the Unexplored

Beyond the hills where whispers call,
Lies a realm where shadows fall.
Rivers twist in secret scrolls,
Untamed lands cradle hidden souls.

Mountains rise with ancient grace,
Guarding paths we dare not trace.
A wildflower blooms, bright and rare,
In places few would ever dare.

Reflections in Dim Light

In twilight's glow, the world unfolds,
Stories waiting to be told.
Mirrors flicker, shadows play,
Haunting echoes lead the way.

Glimmers dance on surfaces wet,
Whispers linger, minds beget.
Each thought a glint, a fleeting spark,
In the silence, deep and dark.

Enigmas of the Beyond

Stars align in cryptic signs,
Secrets woven through the pines.
Galaxies hum a distant tune,
As night unveils the silver moon.

Questions linger in the air,
What lies waiting, unaware?
With every step, a riddle grows,
In the depth where no one goes.

Mysteries of the Unfamiliar

Veils of mist in the morning's rise,
Hide the truth from curious eyes.
Footprints lead to paths untried,
In the stillness, dreams abide.

Forgotten tales of lives once lived,
Whispers of what one could give.
A fleeting glance at what's inside,
Unfamiliar worlds, where wonders bide.

The Forgotten Chronicles

In a dusty tome, the tales unfold,
Whispers of heroes, brave and bold.
Pages yellow, ink begins to fade,
Memories linger, in shadows laid.

Once vibrant lives now shadows cast,
Echoes of laughter, a haunting past.
With every turn, the stories breathe,
In the silence, we weave and grieve.

A journey lost on paths not tread,
Through realms of dreams and words unsaid.
The chronicles wait with open arms,
To rekindle lost warmth, forgotten charms.

Nocturnes of the Untouched

Underneath the velvet skies,
Silent whispers, soft and shy.
Stars awaken, secrets sway,
Night embraces, hush the day.

In the moonlight, shadows dance,
Dreamers lost in trance-like stance.
Echoes of a world unheard,
In the silence, hearts are stirred.

Veils of darkness, beauty shines,
In the quiet, magic twines.
As the nightdeep sings its song,
We find where we truly belong.

Crystals in the Ether

Glimmers soft in endless night,
Fragments of dreams, pure delight.
Spread like wings, they rise and fall,
In the ether, they softly call.

Shards of past in twilight glow,
Hopes and wishes, seeds we sow.
Each crystal holds a story dear,
A world embraced, yet far from here.

In stillness, they reveal their grace,
Veils of time in sacred space.
Catch a glimpse, let your heart stir,
In the silence, feel the whisper.

Reveries of the Obscured

In the shadows, dreams entwine,
Visions dance on paths divine.
Hidden thoughts, like spirits roam,
In the quiet, they find home.

Flickers of light in veils of gray,
Secrets linger, fade away.
Through the mist, a soft embrace,
In reveries, we find our place.

Like the twilight, dusk shall blend,
Whispered stories never end.
In the obscured, we seek to find,
A tapestry of heart and mind.

Murmurs of a Dreaming Universe

Stars hum softly in the night,
Galaxies spin in gentle light.
Comets dance through timeless skies,
While secrets linger in their sighs.

In shadows deep, the echoes play,
Time drifts forth, then slips away.
Nebulae paint their tales so bright,
Whispering dreams in velvet night.

Planets whisper, tales untold,
Of ancient myths and dreams of old.
Through cosmic winds, their voices glide,
As dreams unfold in endless tide.

Among the void, we find our place,
In the heart of time and space.
Murmurs wrap us, soft and clear,
In this universe, we hold dear.

Hidden Landscapes

Beneath the surface, shadows creep,
In buried woods where secrets sleep.
Branches twist and grasses sway,
Guarding whispers of the day.

Rivers carve through ancient stone,
In hidden paths, we walk alone.
Echoes linger in cool, damp air,
As nature cradles every care.

Mountains rise with silent grace,
Sheltering tales of time and place.
Each peak holds a breath of lore,
In hidden realms we long to explore.

Through thickets thick, and valleys wide,
Life unfolds, a gentle guide.
In every shadow, life redeems,
Exploring fields of hidden dreams.

Whispers of the Unseen

In silence grows a soft refrain,
A subtle voice amidst the rain.
Listen close, the world will speak,
In hidden ways, the thoughts we seek.

The rustle of leaves, a gentle breeze,
Carries secrets through the trees.
Nature whispers, clear and pure,
Of ancient souls that still endure.

Beneath the veils of night and day,
The unseen paths will gently sway.
Echoes linger, soft and light,
In whispered tones that spark the night.

Awakening the heart and soul,
In every sound, we find our role.
Whispers call from deep within,
A dance of life, where dreams begin.

Echoes of Forgotten Dreams

In the corners of the night,
Echoes flutter, lost from sight.
Whispers float on a weary breath,
Carrying tales of love and death.

Once bright flames now smolder low,
Pulsing rhythms of long ago.
Faded visions in silent screams,
Linger softly in repressed dreams.

The world remembers, still and clear,
Shadows dance with threads of fear.
Time unwinds the knots of fate,
Haunting memories don't abate.

Yet in this gloom, hope does gleam,
For light can spark a fleeting dream.
Echoes call us from the past,
Inviting us to dream at last.

Unseen Horizons

Beyond the veil of fading light,
Where dreams awaken from their flight,
A whisper calls to hearts that yearn,
For secrets held in time's great turn.

The colors dance upon the breeze,
Inviting us to bend our knees,
To gaze upon the distant glow,
Where hope resides, and rivers flow.

Each step we take, unknown and bold,
Guides us through stories yet untold,
Unseen horizons stretch afar,
A promise wrapped in every star.

In twilight's hush, the world unspun,
We chase the shadow of the sun,
And find in every fading hue,
A glimpse of dreams that might come true.

Labyrinths of Light and Shadow

In corners dark where silence stirs,
A dance of light, a secret whirs,
The pathways wind, a twisting maze,
Each turn revealing hidden ways.

The flicker of a fading spark,
Illuminates the cold and dark,
Where shadows play their muted game,
And light takes on a different name.

We wander through this brave expanse,
Embracing shadows, finding chance,
For in each step, a truth does hide,
A paradox where worlds collide.

Labyrinths of secrets weave,
A tapestry we dare believe,
In every twist, a chance to find,
The mirror of our searching mind.

Letters from a Hidden Shore

Upon the sands where whispers dwell,
I find the echoes, soft and swell,
Words etched in waves, a story told,
Of love and loss, of dreams, of gold.

Each letter kissed by ocean's grace,
A message lost in time and space,
Beneath the moon's enchanted gaze,
The shoreline holds its timeless ways.

Seagulls cry with secrets deep,
As tides pull forth the thoughts I keep,
With every wave, new tales arise,
A symphony beneath the skies.

From hidden shores, the whispers roam,
Inviting hearts to feel at home,
And in these letters, truths align,
A bridge from heart to heart—divine.

Whims of the Unfathomable

In depths where dreams and wishes blend,
The unfathomable has no end,
It dances lightly, airy, free,
A wisp of thought, a mystery.

The tides of time, they swirl and swoop,
A playful dance, a cosmic loop,
Each whim that flows, a fleeting glance,
An echo of a timeless dance.

Through veils of doubt, through mists of fear,
Each heartbeat whispers what is near,
In wonder's grasp, we lose our way,
Yet find the light in shades of gray.

The unfathomable calls our name,
With every twist, a chance to claim,
The beauty found in what's unknown,
A fleeting thought, a love once sown.

The Otherworldly Odyssey

In realms where shadows dance and play,
The stars align in a mystic sway,
Whispers of dreams drift in the night,
Guiding lost souls toward the light.

Through forests deep and rivers wide,
Where ancient whispers dare to bide,
A journey calls, a heart ignites,
In the embrace of celestial sights.

Mountains loom, a daunting crest,
Yet hope blooms bright within the chest,
Each step a tale, each breath a chance,
To lose oneself in the cosmic dance.

Upon a ship of silver beams,
We sail across the ocean of dreams,
With every wave, a new refrain,
An odyssey through joy and pain.

A Passage Through the Unimagined

Beyond the veil of known confines,
Where time ticks slow and fate entwines,
A passage waits, old as the stars,
Awaiting those who bear their scars.

With unseen doors that softly creak,
And echoes of the voices speak,
Winds carry tales from worlds unknown,
Inviting hearts to find their own.

In the embrace of void and light,
We chase the dawn, abandon night,
Each step we take, a spark ignites,
In realms unbound, where hope excites.

As thoughts become the threads we weave,
In fabric spun from what we believe,
A journey forged in dreams profound,
In whispers deep, our truth is found.

Echoes from an Invisible Realm

In silence hangs a symphony,
Of echoes soft, of mystery,
Invisible threads that bind us tight,
In shadowed realms beyond our sight.

A flicker here, a shadow there,
Whispers dance upon the air,
In every heartbeat, every sigh,
Resonates the unseen sky.

Through labyrinths of thought we tread,
Where spirit guides and senses spread,
Each echo tells a tale of time,
A rhythm pure, a silent rhyme.

As we listen, hearts will soar,
To places known, yet never more,
In echoes sweet, our souls ignite,
In invisible realms, pure and bright.

The Path Not Taken

Upon the fork where choices lie,
A whisper beckons, soft as sigh,
Two roads diverge in morning light,
One dark as night, the other bright.

With every step, a tale unfolds,
Of dreams we chase and tales untold,
The path not taken ever glows,
In secret glades where wonder grows.

Yet doubts may linger, shadows loom,
In twilight's grasp, we feel the gloom,
But courage whispers, strong and clear,
The road less traveled draws us near.

So choose we must, with hearts ablaze,
To seek the light in tangled maze,
For in the choice, the spirit wakes,
And life begins where courage makes.

Fourteen Steps to Nowhere

The path entwines, a twist of fate,
With each step taken, we hesitate.
A door appears, yet leads to gray,
Echoes whisper, then fade away.

Time slips past, like sand through hands,
In shadows cast, the silence stands.
A fleeting glance at dreams once bright,
Now lost within an endless night.

Each corner turned, the void awaits,
A journey long that tempts and prates.
Fourteen steps on paths unclear,
A quest that lingers, year by year.

Yet in the dark, a spark ignites,
A fleeting hope that dares to rise.
To nowhere bound, we search for light,
In the depths of the endless night.

Riddles Wrapped in Ghosts

Whispers flitter through the air,
Unseen faces, secrets bare.
The moonlight dances on the ground,
In every shadow, riddles found.

Lost voices call from ages past,
Their echoes linger, deep and vast.
A puzzle formed in shadows' play,
With every clue, they slip away.

Fingers trace on walls of stone,
The stories told, but not our own.
A fleeting thought, a chilling breeze,
Riddles wrapped in memories.

From ghostly realms, they pull us near,
Each question raised, a hidden fear.
Unraveling threads of time unseen,
In haunted tales, we glean what's been.

Fragments of the Unknown

Scattered pieces on the floor,
Shattered dreams we can't ignore.
In every shard, a story waits,
Of whispered hopes and twisted fates.

The night conceals what's yet to show,
Fragments shine with a subtle glow.
Unseen wonders in the dark,
The longing heart begins to spark.

A journey leads through misty streams,
Through fleeting visions and broken dreams.
Each fragment holds a whispered tale,
A path unknown where shadows pale.

Let pieces join to form a map,
Of past and present, time's own trap.
In the unknown, we find our way,
Through fragments lost, to light of day.

The Silence of Starlit Plains

Beneath the vast, unending sky,
Where distant stars like dreams float by.
The silence wraps the earth in peace,
In starlit nights, all worries cease.

A gentle breeze, a whisper low,
Carries secrets only night can know.
Each twinkle speaks of worlds afar,
In the stillness, we glimpse a star.

The canvas spread in shades of blue,
Infinite tales that feel so true.
While silence reigns, our hearts take flight,
In the glow of the starry night.

Embraced by dark, yet feeling bright,
The silence sings, a pure delight.
In starlit plains, our spirits roam,
In the vast expanse, we find our home.

The Dance of the Unseen

Whispers in the twilight air,
Shadows sway without a care.
Footsteps echo on the ground,
Silence wraps the night around.

Stars align in secret grace,
In the dark, they find their place.
A dance crafted by the night,
Invisible to human sight.

Breath of wind, a fleeting touch,
Magic woven in the hush.
Through the veil, they twist and glide,
In the dark, they always hide.

Eyes may close, yet dreams can see,
The beauty that will always be.
In the unseen, we take our chance,
Joined forever in the dance.

Threads of the Cosmic Weave

A tapestry of stars unfurls,
In the night, the heavens swirl.
Threads of fate and time combine,
In this vast, grand design.

Each thread holds a story deep,
Woven pathways that we keep.
Nebulae in vibrant bloom,
Whisper secrets through the gloom.

Across the void, connections spark,
Light and dark in endless arc.
In every thread, a pulse of life,
Weaving joy and woven strife.

From the cosmos, we emerge,
As diverse dreams start to surge.
Intertwined, forever free,
In the weave of destiny.

Echoes from Dreams of Old

Time spills forth from distant lore,
Memories linger at the shore.
In the twilight, echoes sigh,
Bringing whispers from the sky.

Fragments dance in moonlit streams,
Carried forth on faded beams.
Voices call through shadows dim,
Timeless songs that never grim.

Through the mists of ages past,
We find the stories that will last.
Each echo carries ancient weight,
Binding us to what was fated.

In the stillness, hearts can learn,
To listen well, for candles burn.
From dreams of old, we gather light,
In echoes, find our strength to fight.

Reflections in the Abyss

Glimmers surface from the deep,
A dance where shadows softly creep.
In the water, visions swirl,
As dark secrets start to unfurl.

Faces change with every wave,
In the abyss, we learn to brave.
What is lost must find its way,
Through the depths, come what may.

A mirror holds both dark and light,
In its depths, we seek our sight.
With every ripple, truths collide,
In reflections, hearts confide.

Facing fears, we touch the void,
In the silence, we're employed.
Reflections form in dark caress,
In the abyss, we find our rest.

Visions from the Abyss

In darkened depths where shadows creep,
Silent whispers weave and sweep.
Echoes of dreams long left behind,
In the abyss, what will we find?

Figures dance in the midnight haze,
Fragments lost in the twilight phase.
They beckon with a haunting call,
Will we rise, or choose to fall?

Wisps of light, a fleeting chance,
In this place, we dare to glance.
Through the murk, a path appears,
Guided by our hopes and fears.

From the deep, our spirits soar,
Confronting myths and ancient lore.
In visions bright, the truth persists,
Floating forever in the mist.

The Forgotten Tapestry

Threads of gold and hues so bright,
Woven tales in fading light.
Stories lost in time's embrace,
In the tapestry, we find our place.

Once revered, now torn and frayed,
In every stitch, memories played.
Silken whispers of love and pain,
In each pattern, a lingering stain.

Will we mend what time has torn?
Bring to life what was forlorn?
With gentle hands, we dare to sew,
A story rich, with threads aglow.

Underneath the shrouded veil,
Midst trails of dust where shadows wail.
We cherish all that time has shown,
In this fabric, we are not alone.

Fables from the Fringe

In the shadows where few dare wander,
Lies a world ripe with tales to ponder.
Creatures glide on whispers low,
Secrets held in the moonlight's glow.

Through the tangled, twisted trees,
Echoes float on the midnight breeze.
Fables crafted from dusk till dawn,
In the fringe, the myths are drawn.

Chimeras dance beneath the stars,
Bathed in light from distant cars.
With every tale, a truth recedes,
And from the fringe, each vision feeds.

Journey forth into the strange,
Where the ordinary meets the change.
With open hearts and curious eyes,
Fables from the fringe will rise.

A Symphony of Unwritten Tales

In silence rests a tale untold,
In every heart, a world of gold.
Each moment drips with possibility,
A symphony of what can be.

Every breath a note in time,
Crafting verses without rhyme.
In our minds, the stories flow,
Like rivers winding, deep and slow.

Unwritten pages, dreams unchained,
In whispered sighs, hope is gained.
Compose the songs of joy and strife,
A symphony that breathes with life.

As we dance on the edge of fate,
Let our spirits communicate.
For every story waits its call,
In unwritten tales, we find it all.

Threads of the Unknown

In shadows deep, where whispers grow,
Threads of the unknown, gently flow.
They weave a tale, both dark and bright,
Guiding the lost through endless night.

The heart beats soft, a secret sigh,
Beneath the stars, where echoes lie.
Each fragile strand, a story spun,
In silent circles, we become one.

Connections made, though unseen hands,
Tugging at dreams, across the lands.
Invisible ties that bind us close,
Threads of the unknown, we love the most.

Through twisting paths, the journey calls,
A dance of fate, as shadow falls.
We walk the line, both brave and bold,
In threads of the unknown, truths unfold.

The Enigma of Silent Seas

The silent seas, a mystic dome,
Whispers hidden, a beckoning home.
Waves caress the ghostly shore,
In the stillness, secrets soar.

Beneath the calm, the currents churn,
Echoes of tales long since learned.
A ship adrift in moonlit dreams,
Navigates the softest gleams.

Mariners chase the fading light,
Searching for shadows of the night.
The enigma waits, in liquid glass,
Holding memories that come to pass.

Each tide a tale, each breeze a sign,
In the silent seas, where stars align.
Journey forth, let your heart be free,
To unravel the enigma of the sea.

Fantasies in the Twilight

When day succumbs to evening's haze,
Fantasies bloom in twilight's gaze.
Colors blend, a soft embrace,
Whispers linger in this sacred space.

Dreams take flight on silken wings,
Float through realms where magic sings.
Stars awaken in velvet night,
Guiding hearts to lost delight.

In shadows cast, find hidden lore,
Moments fleeting, forevermore.
Each heartbeat thrums in rhythmic time,
Fantasies dance, sublime, divine.

As darkness wraps, let secrets flow,
In twilight's glow, true wonders show.
Embrace the night, let spirits sway,
In fantasies where we wish to stay.

Glimpses of the Invisible

In every breath, a fleeting sight,
Glimpses of the invisible light.
Beyond the veil, shadows play,
Revealing truths that drift away.

The whispers soft, like autumn leaves,
Carry the heart in gentle eves.
A touch unseen, yet felt so real,
Glimpses of dreams that we conceal.

With open minds, we start to see,
The hidden worlds that long to be.
Each fleeting moment, a sacred chance,
To join the dance of life's expanse.

In every silence, a song will rise,
Glimpses of the invisible skies.
Hold tight to hope, let visions flow,
For in the unseen, we come to know.

Visions in the Void

In the dark of night, silence reigned,
Shadows dance lightly, unchained.
Echoes of thoughts drift around,
In the void, lost dreams are found.

Stars whisper secrets, dim yet bright,
Guiding the wanderers through the night.
Veils of mystery, tightly sewn,
In vastness, the heart finds its tone.

Glimmers of hope just out of reach,
Lessons of solitude, they teach.
In the silence, visions unite,
Fleeting glimpses of pure delight.

From the void, a voice so clear,
Calls to the brave who dare to steer.
Into the unknown, boldly they tread,
In the heart of darkness, lights are spread.

Treasures of the Untamed

Among the trees where wild things roam,
Secrets of earth find their home.
Whispers of nature, ancient, wise,
Beneath the sunlit, endless skies.

Rivers dance over stones so old,
Stories of life in water told.
Mountains stand, steadfast and grand,
Guardians of treasures, quiet and planned.

Fields of gold sway in the breeze,
A symphony played by buzzing bees.
In the wild, every moment pure,
Where beauty and chaos find a cure.

Beneath the stars, the spirits sing,
A chorus of joy, nature's spring.
In untamed hearts, adventure brews,
With treasures waiting for us to choose.

Beyond the Fabric of Reality

Threads of time weave tales unseen,
Dimensions shift, in between.
Reality bends, and dreams collide,
In the cosmos, where secrets hide.

Echoes of futures dance and play,
As shadows of past drift away.
Through narrow paths, we traverse wide,
In the realm where visions slide.

Galaxies whisper, stars align,
Fates are spun, in shadows divine.
Beyond the veil, truths start to gleam,
In the twilight of every dream.

Waves of existence quake and sway,
In the fabric of night and day.
What lies beyond, we long to find,
In the realms of the unconfined.

Whispers on the Wind

Through rustling leaves, soft secrets pass,
Carried gently, like flowing glass.
Murmurs of fate, fate yet untold,
With every breeze, new tales unfold.

Songs of the earth in gentle tides,
Nature's voice where harmony abides.
In the chill of dusk, soft sighs blend,
Whispers of hope as shadows extend.

Clouds drift by, painting the skies,
Mirroring dreams where freedom lies.
In every gust, a story spins,
The heart awakens, the spirit wins.

As moonlight bathes the tranquil land,
The whispers call, a gentle hand.
Through night's embrace, our hearts may soar,
On the wind, forevermore.

Whispers of the Unseen

In the quiet night, whispers sway,
Secrets of dreams that gently play.
Beyond the stars, where shadows blend,
Voices linger, for time won't end.

Fleeting glimpses, a soft embrace,
Ethereal forms in a hidden space.
Silent echoes of stories told,
In the dark, where tales unfold.

Every whisper, a tender sigh,
Carried softly, like the sky.
A dance of light, both near and far,
Guided gently by each twinkling star.

Listen closely, let your heart soar,
Whispers of the unseen, forevermore.
In the silence, find your peace,
As hidden wonders never cease.

Echoes from the Veil

Beyond the curtain, echoes ring,
Carried softly on the wing.
Through the mist, where shadows creep,
Ancient secrets, buried deep.

Reverberations of times gone by,
Stirring softly like a sigh.
Each sound a memory, timeless grace,
Veiled fragments in an endless chase.

In the stillness, a tale remains,
Woven stories in earthly chains.
From the past, we learn to rise,
Echoing truth beneath the skies.

Listen intently to what they say,
Echoes from the veil lead the way.
In their whispers, the lost is found,
A hidden world where dreams abound.

Shadows Beyond the Known

In the twilight, shadows play,
Dancing lightly, drifting away.
Where the light has yet to tread,
Mysteries linger, left unsaid.

Through the veil of night, they roam,
Seeking solace, a place called home.
In the silence, they softly creep,
Guarding secrets, buried deep.

Shadows whisper in twilight's grace,
Hiding tales in a sacred space.
Beyond the known, what's yet to see,
A realm of wonders, wild and free.

Open your heart, and take a chance,
Join the shadows in their dance.
Where fear dissolves and dreams ignite,
In the dark, we find our light.

Secrets of the Hidden World

Veiled in silence, secrets sleep,
In the forest, where shadows creep.
Gentle rustles, a fleeting sound,
Whispers of life, profound and bound.

In the depths, where few may tread,
A tapestry of life is spread.
Roots entwined in sacred lore,
Stories untold from times of yore.

Every leaf, a page of fate,
Holding wisdom that won't abate.
With each step, we weave the thread,
Secrets awaken, love widespread.

Listen closely, let your spirit soar,
Discover the hidden, forevermore.
In this world, where shadows blend,
Secrets embrace, as time transcends.

Mystical Pathways Untraveled

In twilight's glow, the paths unfold,
Where secrets whisper, stories told.
Beneath the stars, old dreams arise,
And dance with shadows in the skies.

Each step a heartbeat, faint yet clear,
Guided by wisdom, drawing near.
With every turn, a choice to make,
A journey born from dawn's sweet wake.

Echoes of laughter, spirits play,
Leading the lost along the way.
Through tangled woods and silver streams,
The heart finds solace in its dreams.

Songs of the Night's Embrace

The moonlit glow reflects the night,
As stars above shimmer so bright.
Soft whispers float on gentle air,
A serenade of sweet despair.

Crickets chirp a lullaby,
As shadows dance and spirits fly.
In twilight's arms, we find our peace,
A moment's pause, a sweet release.

Wrapped in silence, wrapped in sighs,
The universe in stillness lies.
Each breath we take a borrowed gift,
In night's embrace, our hearts will lift.

Across the Sea of Shadows

In blackened waves, the shadows swim,
Where light once danced on hopeful whim.
Caught in a tide of dark desires,
The echoes fade, the silence fires.

With weary sails, we seek the shore,
To find what lies forevermore.
A journey carved in dreams and fears,
Through whispered winds and hidden tears.

Yet in the depths, a spark remains,
A light that breaks through bitter chains.
Across the sea, new worlds await,
Where shadows part and hope holds fate.

Chasing the Invisible

In quiet corners, shadows wane,
We seek the unseen, feel the strain.
With every heartbeat, every breath,
We chase the whispers, dance with death.

Beyond the veil where visions tread,
We wander paths the wise have led.
In ghostly halls where echoes call,
The invisible binds us one and all.

Fleeting moments, shifts of light,
We reach for dreams that take to flight.
In chasing what we cannot see,
We find ourselves, we roam so free.

Floating in Forgotten Realities

In dreams we drift and soar,
Through realms unseen and unknown.
Whispers of a silent lore,
Where shadows dwell, seeds are sown.

Clouded visions, lost in flight,
Moments blur, fading glows.
Chasing echoes through the night,
Each lost thread gently flows.

Forgotten tales in faded light,
Woven into the fabric of time.
Caught in the web of endless fright,
A dance with silence, a silent rhyme.

In this space where we convene,
The heart beats in timeless grace.
Floating soft in worlds unseen,
Embracing dreams in this hidden place.

Murmurs from the Beyond

Echoes linger in the mist,
Voices calling, never clear.
Fractured dreams we can't resist,
Whispers swirl, drawing near.

Unseen hands that gently guide,
Through the dark, we weave our way.
In this realm, where shadows hide,
Murmurs lead us, come what may.

Branches twist, the night grows deep,
Moonlight dances on the grass.
Ancient secrets that we keep,
Bound by the threads of the past.

In the silence, truths collide,
A tapestry of fear and dream.
We stand still, hearts open wide,
Listening close to the unseen stream.

Timeless Tales of Uncertainty

Every tick a story spins,
Life unfolds in shades of gray.
Moments lost, yet still it begins,
Questions linger, lead us astray.

Paths diverge, a forked embrace,
Fates entwined, but which to choose?
In the dance of time and space,
Certainty gives way to blues.

Fleeting whispers, time's cruel jest,
Holding on as shadows sway.
In this quest, we seek the best,
Grasping hope with each delay.

Tales of joy and sorrow weave,
Curved in mystery, poised for flight.
In each heartbeat, we believe,
The light can conquer endless night.

The Colors We Can't See

In the realm of hidden hues,
Palettes breathe and softly sigh.
Brushstrokes dance with secret views,
A canvas rich, yet shy.

Glimmers hide in twilight's fold,
Vibrance whispers, slow and sweet.
Stories in the silence told,
In every shadow, shades retreat.

Blues and greens in silent plight,
Dreams that shimmer out of reach.
Colors fade in the fading light,
Lessons linger, shapes to teach.

Yet in this void, we strive to find,
A spectrum bright but veiled in gray.
The unseen realms where hearts entwined,
Breathe beauty in their hidden sway.

Hues of the Forgotten

In the twilight of fading dreams,
Whispers paint the silent seams.
Colors blend in a muted dance,
Life's canvas left to chance.

Echoes linger, soft and low,
Secrets of the past bestow.
Most vibrant shades turn to gray,
As memories drift away.

Sunrise might not break the night,
Yet shadows hold a softer light.
In every hue, a tale untold,
The warmth of love, now cold.

In this realm where silence calls,
Blanket memories on old walls.
Hues once bright, now dimly glow,
In the heart of those who know.

Shadows of the Unmapped

Wandering paths we dare not tread,
Maps of the lost, pages unread.
Footsteps echo on gravel stones,
In the twilight, ghosts atones.

Uncharted dreams, like currents flow,
Into the depths where few dare go.
Skyless realms, where shadows creep,
Every secret sown to keep.

Murmurs rise from hidden trails,
Ancient whispers tell their tales.
In this maze, lost souls collide,
While the stars choose to abide.

Tracing lines in the unseen,
Feel the pulse of spaces keen.
Here beneath the moon's soft glow,
Unmapped lives begin to flow.

Glimpses into the Void

In the stillness of the night,
Fragments flicker, dimming light.
Eyes that search for what's beyond,
In the silence, we respond.

Visions dance just out of reach,
Lessons that the stars might teach.
In the void, truths lay bare,
Frozen moments, chilled air.

Annals of the past unfold,
Tales of hope wrapped in gold.
Yet the shadows veil the way,
To the dawn of a new day.

Glimpses spark the soul's deep fire,
In the heart, dreams conspire.
Brushing wings of destiny,
In the void, we learn to be.

Echoes from the Lost

Faint whispers through the tangled trees,
Traditions caught in the breeze.
Footprints fade under layers of dust,
Memories held in ancient rust.

Time bends low where secrets lie,
Underneath the vast, dark sky.
Voices merge in a soft refrain,
Echoes of joy, sorrow, and pain.

In forgotten halls of stone,
Silent dreams call out alone.
But in the quiet, they persist,
Pulse of the past cannot be missed.

Through layers deep, the stories flow,
Holding truths we yearn to know.
In echoes from the lost we find,
The threads that bind all humankind.

Shades of Dreams Yet to Bloom

In the garden of wishes, soft whispers sigh,
Petals unfurl, reaching toward the sky.
Colors of hope dance, gentle and light,
As dawn brings the promise, banishing night.

Each bud holds a secret, a vision untold,
Cradling the stories of dreams bright and bold.
In the warmth of the sun, they lean and they sway,
Painting the world in a shimmering gray.

Roots deep in the earth, they're anchored with care,
Nurtured by love, in the cool morning air.
In the tapestry woven of moments long past,
Shades of our dreams flicker, forever to last.

Through seasons of change, they flourish and grow,
Waiting for moments when courage will show.
In the heart of tomorrow, where visions align,
Shades of dreams yet to bloom silently shine.

A Celestial Journey

Stars like lanterns, lighting the way,
Guiding the soul through night into day.
Planets in motion, a dance so divine,
Tracing the patterns of space in a line.

Galaxies whisper with voices so clear,
Echoes of ages that only we hear.
Nebulas blossom, with colors that sing,
Painting the canvas of life on a wing.

Comets with tails leave trails of bright fire,
Stirring the heart with a longing desire.
Cosmic winds sweep across endless plains,
Carrying dreams in their ethereal chains.

Through the vast expanse, our spirits will soar,
Finding new worlds, forever to explore.
A celestial journey in twilight's embrace,
Woven with stardust, a boundless grace.

The Forgotten Grove of Spirits

In the heart of the woods where shadows reside,
Whispers of legends and spirits abide.
Trees stand as sentinels, ancient and wise,
Guarding the secrets beneath emerald skies.

Moss-covered stones tell a tale of the past,
Echoes of laughter, a world unsurpassed.
In the stillness of twilight, a shimmer ignites,
Memories linger in the soft silver lights.

Ghostly apparitions drift through the air,
Veils of the past weave a mystical snare.
Time weaves a tapestry, frayed at the seams,
Revealing the stories that linger in dreams.

In this forgotten grove, the lost find their way,
Guided by spirits who gently convey,
That though we may wander, we're never alone,
For the hearts of the lost will always be known.

Unfolding the Fabric of Dreams

In the loom of the night where visions are spun,
Threads of our hopes in the darkness run.
Each shimmer a promise, each shadow a chance,
Unfolding the fabric, our lives in a dance.

Tapestries woven with colors so bright,
Glimmers of futures tucked out of sight.
Every stitch whispers a tale yet to be,
Binding the moments and setting them free.

As dawn breaks the silence, the patterns emerge,
A symphony crafted from every sweet surge.
In the heart of the dreamscape, the weaver stands tall,
With hands full of stories, they cradle them all.

Unraveling visions like clouds in the skies,
Revealing the truths behind our every sigh.
Through the rhythms of life, we're drawn in the seam,
Unfolding the fabric, the essence of dream.

Tales from the Abyss

In shadows deep, where whispers dwell,
Secrets lie in the ocean's swell.
Forgotten dreams, and sunken cries,
Awakened now, they surface, rise.

Darkness weaves its eerie song,
Guiding souls that drift along.
With tales of shipwrecked hearts in tow,
The abyss beckons, soft and low.

Ancient mariners lost their way,
Their ghosts linger, night and day.
Echoes of the deep resound,
In watery graves, their fates are found.

From depths unseen, a story flows,
In every wave, the tide bestows.
Life and death meld, entwined in grace,
The abyss holds a sacred space.

Visions of the Invisible

Beneath the veil, where spirits roam,
Hidden realms call us back home.
In misty hues, perceptions blend,
Life's true essence, our hearts defend.

Fleeting glimpses, shadows play,
Unseen forces guide our way.
With every breath, the whispers sing,
Of truths concealed and hidden things.

In stillness found, we see the light,
Invisible threads weave day and night.
A tapestry of dreams and fear,
Unseen wonders linger near.

The cosmos speaks in subtle signs,
Connecting all with gentle lines.
In silence, we begin to find,
The visions of the heart and mind.

Wonders of the Unrevealed

In twilight's grasp, a mystery brews,
Unrevealed wonders, ancient views.
Time stands still as secrets bloom,
In shadows cast, yet light in gloom.

The universe whispers, soft and low,
In every star, a tale to show.
Hidden realms, where dreams take flight,
Unseen magic dances in the night.

From depths of earth to skies of blue,
Life unfolds in shades anew.
Mysteries linger, just out of sight,
In pursuit of truth, we ignite.

In silence, we seek what lies beyond,
With open hearts, of which we're fond.
The wonders of the world concealed,
Are treasures found, once revealed.

Chronicles of the Silent

Beneath the stillness, stories weave,
In every pause, the heart believes.
Silent whispers, ancient lore,
Chronicles of those who explore.

In quiet moments, truths unfold,
The silent tales that yet are told.
Each heartbeat echoes, faint yet clear,
A testament to all we hold dear.

From seasons past to futures bright,
In hushed tones, we find the light.
Memories linger, softly blend,
The chronicles where paths transcend.

In the silence, we find our peace,
A gentle strength that will not cease.
Through time and space, we journey on,
In chronicles of the dusk and dawn.

Worlds Behind Closed Eyes

In the silence, dreams take flight,
Whispers of stars in the dark of night.
Colors bloom in vibrant hues,
Painting tales that time renews.

Softly drift where shadows play,
Guided by hope, we find our way.
Each heartbeat is a secret shared,
A universe within us, bared.

Beyond the gaze, where visions flow,
In this haven, we come to know.
Eclipsing fears, we break the chains,
In worlds unseen, love remains.

With every blink, a story we weave,
In closed eyes, our souls believe.
Through realms of wonder, we arise,
In the silence, worlds surprise.

A Journey Through the Unspoken

Words unspoken linger near,
In heartbeats deep, we draw so near.
Silent sighs, a language true,
Where echoes dance, we find the view.

Through uncharted paths we roam,
Seeking solace, finding home.
In the depths of silent grace,
We discover our hidden place.

Every glance, a story told,
With silent threads, our lives unfold.
In the stillness, whispers soar,
Connecting us forevermore.

In the silence, we embrace,
A journey through the unspoken space.
Hand in hand, we learn and grow,
In the quiet, love will show.

Ethereal Echoes

Out in the void, where spirits blend,
Ethereal echoes softly send.
Melodies rise, a haunting sound,
In the night, their whispers found.

Light as air, they weave through time,
A dance of thoughts, a perfect rhyme.
Each note a thread, a bond we share,
In echoes, love hangs in the air.

Silent moments, where dreams reside,
Ethereal whispers as our guide.
In twilight's grasp, our spirits meet,
In endless echoes, love's heartbeat.

Woven together, we drift and sway,
In ethereal echoes that never fray.
Through the night, we find our light,
In shared whispers, we unite.

Through the Misty Veil

Wanders lost, in fog so deep,
Through the mist, our secrets keep.
Veils of magic, softly dance,
In each breath, we seize our chance.

Shadows flicker, shapes entwine,
In the murmur, hearts align.
Glimmers faint, a guiding hand,
Through the misty veil, we stand.

Whispers tease like gentle rain,
In the haze, we shed our pain.
Step by step, we break the mold,
Through the fog, our truths unfold.

With courage found, we journey on,
Through the misty veil at dawn.
In this place of dreams, we sway,
Together, we'll find our way.

Paths of Forgotten Dreams

In shadows deep, where whispers fade,
Lost echoes trace the dreams we made.
Each step we take on this worn road,
Holds tales of hope, and hearts once glowed.

The stars above, so far and bright,
Guide us through the silent night.
With every twist, the past unveils,
A journey woven with unseen trails.

Beneath the weight of endless time,
We carry forth a silent chime.
Each sigh of wind, a soft embrace,
Reviving dreams in this sacred place.

As dawn approaches, shades will fall,
Yet in our hearts, we hear the call.
For every dream that's lost in haze,
Awakens hope in brighter days.

Journeys into the Uncharted

With compass set and sails unfurled,
We venture forth into the world.
Unknown horizons stretch ahead,
Where every path holds tales unsaid.

The wind, a friend, beckons us near,
As we chase visions, quell our fear.
Each wave a story, strong and bold,
In depths of blue, new dreams behold.

Stars above like diamonds gleam,
Illuminating each hidden dream.
Through valleys vast and mountains steep,
We tread the lands where secrets sleep.

In every grain of sand we find,
The whispers of a curious mind.
Embrace the journey, seek the light,
For every step ignites our flight.

Lullabies of the Unwritten

In quiet corners, stories wait,
With dreams of love and twists of fate.
Unwritten words, soft as a sigh,
They dance on pages yet to fly.

Beneath the moon's gentle embrace,
Ideas awaken, find their place.
A melody hums in the still air,
Whispers of hope, beyond compare.

The heart's sweet song longs to be told,
In verses bright, visions unfold.
Through ink and pen, the magic grows,
As every thought, the spirit knows.

So hold these dreams, let silence reign,
For in the stillness, there's no pain.
The lullabies of lives not crossed,
Remind us all of dreams not lost.

The Unfathomable Horizon

Beyond the edge where visions blur,
The horizon waits, full of allure.
With eyes wide open, hearts on fire,
We chase the dawn, igniting desire.

Clouds drift softly, painting the sky,
As we ponder what dreams may lie.
A canvas vast, with colors bright,
Awaits the brush of endless light.

In every glance, the future gleams,
With every heartbeat, pulse of dreams.
The path ahead, though steep and grand,
Calls forth courage to take a stand.

As twilight beckons, shadows blend,
We seek the truths that never end.
For in the vastness, hope will shine,
Guiding hearts along the line.

Stories Yet to Be Told

In the quiet of the night,
Dreams linger soft and bright.
Whispers echo through the air,
Tales of wonder, joy, and care.

Pages turn in fading light,
Journeys start with every flight.
Hearts are woven, threads of gold,
In the stories yet to be told.

Beneath the stars, we find our way,
Lost in moments, come what may.
Each memory a gem to hold,
In the stories yet to be told.

Let the future raise its hand,
We'll write our fates upon the sand.
With every moment, life unfolds,
In the stories yet to be told.

Mysteries in the Mist

Veils of gray dance in the dawn,
Nature's secrets slowly drawn.
Footsteps echo where shadows play,
Whispers calling, come what may.

In the depths where silence dwells,
Hidden stories, ancient spells.
The air is thick with tales untold,
Mysteries wrapped in legends old.

Fog descends upon the ground,
In each corner, dreams abound.
Through the haze, a vision stirs,
A gentle sigh, the world concurs.

Searching hearts in twilight's glow,
Follow paths where few dare go.
In the mist, the truth unfolds,
Mysteries waiting to be told.

The Veil of Unreality

Beneath the surface, shadows gleam,
A world that dances in a dream.
Flickering lights, a bright charade,
Life's illusions gently fade.

Threads of thought and notions weave,
A tapestry for those who believe.
In this realm where time unbends,
The veil of truth, it twists and bends.

Moments drift like autumn leaves,
In the stories that our heart believes.
Reality, a fragile hold,
Behind the veil, the past unfolds.

In the night, we seek the signs,
Lost in echoes, drawn to lines.
Through the maze of what we see,
The veil of unreality.

Footprints in the Ether

Across the space where echoes blend,
Footprints mark where journeys end.
In the ether, we leave our trace,
Whispers linger, memories embrace.

Stars align with stories bright,
Guiding spirits through the night.
Each step taken, far and near,
Footprints echo, soft but clear.

Moments tethered in the air,
Silent shadows linger there.
Between the realms, we roam so free,
Footprints in the ether, you and me.

In the vastness, dreams collide,
Winding paths where hopes abide.
In every heartbeat, love's endeavor,
Footprints in the ether, always clever.

Canvas of the Unimagined

A brush strokes dreams on silent air,
Colors dance, a wild affair.
Shapes emerge from shadows bright,
Crafting tales of pure delight.

Whispers echo through the haze,
Textures weave in mystic ways.
Visions collide, worlds unite,
In this realm where all take flight.

Stars paint stories, bold and rare,
In a universe beyond compare.
Each hue a promise, every line,
Invites the heart, makes the soul shine.

From thoughts unspoken, magic grows,
Infinite paths where wonder flows.
On this canvas, life expands,
Boundless horizons drawn by hands.

Whims of the Endless Night

The moon curates tales untold,
Casting silver on dreams of old.
In shadows deep, secrets sigh,
As midnight wanders, time slips by.

Stars giggle in the darkened sky,
While cool winds whisper lullabies.
A serenade of soft, low lights,
Guiding hearts through endless nights.

By the waves, the mysteries stir,
With every pulse, a soft whisper.
Moments linger, then take flight,
In the whims of the endless night.

Dreamers dance beneath the glow,
In twilight's embrace, let feelings flow.
Each heartbeat echoes, softly bright,
A symphony played in moon's delight.

Lurkers in the Twilight

In the dusk, shadows softly creep,
Lurkers prowling, secrets they keep.
With eyes like stars, they watch and wait,
Silent figures who weave fate.

Moonlight dances on whispered fears,
Filtering through the tangled years.
Fingers brush the edges thin,
Where twilight's magic does begin.

Their laughter lingers in the breeze,
Drawing stories from ancient trees.
In every rustle, in every sigh,
Echoes of time passing by.

Guardians of the dusk's embrace,
They know the patterns of space.
In the twilight's fold, they bide,
Lurkers in the shadows, side by side.

Beyond the Edge of Knowing

Veils of doubt obscure the light,
Yet hearts soar in the brave night.
Beyond the edge where reason fades,
Existence waits in endless glades.

What lies beyond the stars we see?
A tapestry of destiny.
Threads of fate entwined and spun,
In realms of possibility, we run.

Courage calls from the deep unknown,
In quiet whispers, it has grown.
To seek, to find, to always dare,
To navigate with utmost care.

Beyond the edge, new worlds await,
Awareness sharpens, we elevate.
Together we'll chart what's yet to be,
Unraveling life's great mystery.

Secrets Beneath the Surface

Beneath the waves, whispers dwell,
Hidden mysteries, tales to tell.
Silent shadows drift and sway,
Secrets waiting, night and day.

In depths unseen, dreams entwine,
Colors fade, yet spark divine.
Treasures lost in briny deep,
Guarded by the ocean's keep.

A shipwreck's song, a ghostly tune,
Under the stars, by light of moon.
Echoes linger, softly sigh,
Where olden legends never die.

Unlock the gates, let light pour in,
Dare to dive, let the journey begin.
For what we seek is just below,
In hidden depths, secrets flow.

Beyond the Boundaries

Across the hills where few may roam,
Lies a world that feels like home.
Paths untraveled, skies so wide,
In the wild, dreams collide.

Mountains rise, the sun aglow,
Whispers of wind in a gentle flow.
Nature beckons, calls your name,
Adventure waits, never the same.

Beyond the fields, the rivers gleam,
Where visions paint a vibrant dream.
Step with courage, leave behind
The chains that bind, the ties that blind.

In every leaf, a story lies,
Under the vast, expansive skies.
Embrace the thrill, let spirits soar,
Beyond the boundaries, seek for more.

Chronicles of the Uncharted

In lands where maps have never traced,
Adventures bloom, life embraced.
Whispers echo through the trees,
Tales are carried by the breeze.

Caves of wonder, skies so clear,
Echoing laughter, freedom near.
Every step, a tale unfolds,
In uncharted realms, bravery molds.

Stars above, a guide so bright,
Charting courses through the night.
Legends form where few have been,
In every heart, courage to win.

Chronicles written in the sand,
Nature's story, vast and grand.
Set your sails, let spirits chase,
For in the unknown lies our place.

Shadows of a Silent World

In the hush of twilight's glow,
Silent whispers start to flow.
Shadows dance on cobblestone,
In this realm, we are alone.

Echoes wane, as moonlight sighs,
Stars awaken in velvet skies.
Each corner hides a secret tale,
Where silence weaves a fragile veil.

Footsteps soft on ancient trails,
As nightingale's sweet song prevails.
Bridges blend of past and now,
Where hearts remember, none allow.

In this quiet, depth resides,
Where the soul in stillness hides.
Shadows linger, tales unsung,
In the silent world, we're young.

Embracing the Unknown

In shadows deep where fears reside,
A whisper calls, I cannot hide.
The road ahead, it twists and bends,
With every step, new life begins.

The stars above, they guide my way,
Through darkened nights and brightened day.
With courage raised, I take a chance,
To dance with fate, to dream, to glance.

Each choice I make, a thread I weave,
In tapestry of those who believe.
A journey vast, an open heart,
Embracing all, I play my part.

Through every doubt, through every fear,
The unknown calls, its voice so clear.
I take a breath, I step outside,
Embracing all, I shall abide.

The Lure of Forgotten Places

In whispers lost, the echoes fade,
To secret paths where dreams are laid.
Old stones hold tales of days gone by,
Beneath the stars, they seem to sigh.

The forest thick, with shadows cast,
Where time stands still, and hearts beat fast.
Each rustling leaf, a story breathes,
In tangled roots, the silence weaves.

The river bends, a gentle flow,
To lands forgotten, where few would go.
With every step, the past awakes,
In sacred silence, the earth partakes.

A haunting tune, a siren's call,
To places lost, that memory recalls.
With open eyes, I wander free,
Exploring realms of mystery.

The Lattice of Undiscovered Lands

Across the seas, where sunlight spills,
Lies hidden dreams, where wonder thrills.
With sails unfurled, the winds will guide,
To shores unknown, to worlds inside.

The mountains rise, so proud and high,
Their peaks embrace the endless sky.
In valleys deep, secrets unfold,
In whispered tales, the brave are bold.

A map unwritten, a quest unframed,
In every heartbeat, adventure claimed.
Through tangled woods and starlit nights,
The spirit soars, the heart ignites.

With every step, the lattice grows,
Of undiscovered lands, it shows.
Together we wander, hand in hand,
Exploring each corner of this grand land.

The Lost Diary of Dreams

In a chest of wood so worn,
A diary waits, dreams forlorn.
Whispers dance on fragile page,
Each word a spark, a hidden sage.

Time has folded, memories freeze,
Promises ride on the autumn breeze.
Stories lost in twilight's glow,
Secrets wrapped in moonlit flow.

Notes of laughter, tears of night,
Echo softly, taking flight.
In the shadows, hopes take form,
Awakening hearts to weather the storm.

Close your eyes, let visions weave,
In the diary, believe, perceive.
Find the dreams you thought were gone,
In the dawn, a brand new song.

Voices in the Wilderness

Whispers rise beneath the trees,
Carried softly by the breeze.
Nature sings, a haunting call,
Echoes through the forest tall.

Lost in thought, the heart takes flight,
Guided by the soft moonlight.
Crisp leaves crunching 'neath my feet,
Paths unseen, where earth and sky meet.

Rivers murmur ancient tales,
Of hidden trails and wind-swept sails.
Creatures stir in dusk's embrace,
Each shadow holds a secret space.

Listen close, the wild one speaks,
Through rustling leaves and mountain peaks.
In wilderness, our spirits blend,
Finding solace, time to mend.

An Enchanted Neverland

In a realm where dreams take flight,
Stars illuminate the endless night.
Fairy wings and laughter blend,
In this place, there's no true end.

Time is lost, forever sways,
As magic paints the skies ablaze.
Watch the whispers of the trees,
Dance along with gentle breeze.

Mermaids sing in sparkling streams,
Where every moment softly gleams.
Pirates roam with hearts so bold,
Adventures waiting to unfold.

In this land of vibrant hues,
Imagination finds its muse.
Every corner holds a story,
A tapestry of timeless glory.

Secrets in the Shadows

In the dark where secrets lie,
Figures move with quiet sighs.
Silhouettes in silence stand,
Lost reflections, hand in hand.

Veils of night cloak all in mystery,
Every echo tells a history.
Footsteps whisper on the ground,
In the shadows, truths are found.

Hidden hearts and whispered dreams,
Flickering like distant beams.
Secrets weave through tangled fate,
In the dusk, we contemplate.

Underneath the watchful moon,
Revelations come, come soon.
The night unveils what's kept apart,
Embracing shadows of the heart.

Milton Keynes UK
Ingram Content Group UK Ltd.
UKHW021936121124
451129UK00007B/116